contents

6 RYAN SAYS 'HI!

8 1995-96 - WHAT A WONDERFUL
SEASON - PART ONE

22 ERIC - THE KING OF OLD TRAFFORD

24 FERGIE - THE BOSS WHO DID THE
DOUBLE TWICE!

26 RYAN'S ROUTINE

28 GIGGSY'S GALLERY

30 MY TEAM-MATES

38 1995-96 - WHAT A WONDERFUL
SEASON - PART TWO

54 THE RYAN GIGGS STORY

60 GIGGSY AT A GLANCE

61 COMPETITION

© 1996 Grandreams Ltd

Written by Ryan Giggs and
Tony Lynch
Designed by Dave Saunders

All facts believed correct at
the time of going to press

Published by Grandreams Ltd
Jadwin House
205-211 Kentish Town Road
London NW5 2JU

Printed in Belgium

Special thanks to Bobby
Charlton's Health & Fitness
Centre, Middleton,
Manchester

Ryan says

...And welcome to the second OFFICIAL RYAN GIGGS ANNUAL from Grandreams, I was really pleased with last year's edition and your reaction to it. This time there's a lot more to celebrate after Manchester United lifted the Premier League trophy for the third time in four seasons AND the FA Cup, making us the first team ever to achieve the 'Double' twice!

This time Grandreams have given us 16 extra pages – which means there are even more great features and superb photographs, taken both on and off the pitch. I especially like the ones that were taken on a snowy day in and around Bobby Charlton's Health & Fitness Centre in Manchester – I hope you do too!

Good luck, best wishes and enjoy your football!

Ryan Giggs

RYAN GIGGS

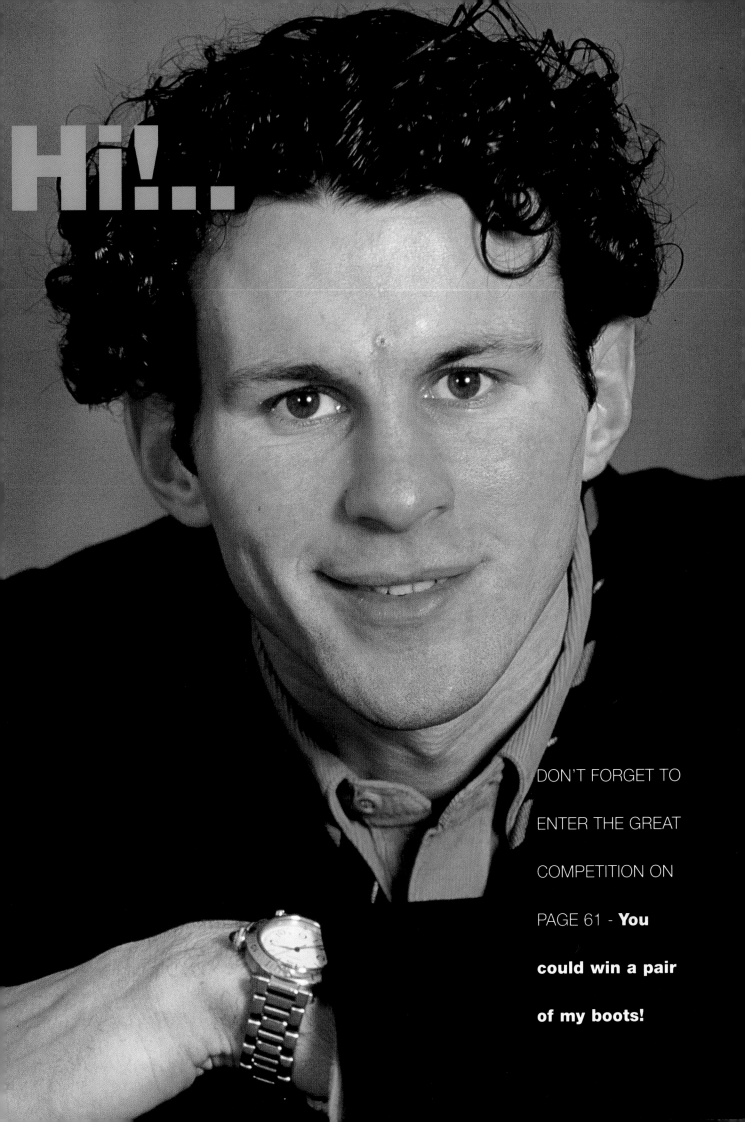

Hi!...

DON'T FORGET TO

ENTER THE GREAT

COMPETITION ON

PAGE 61 - **You**

could win a pair

of my boots!

1995-96 - WHAT A WONDERFUL SEASON -
Part One

Sunday 5 May 1996 will always be a special day for me. It was the last day of the 1995-96 Premier League season. And it was the day when Manchester United beat Middlesbrough 3-0 at the Riverside Stadium - to ensure that a third Premiership title was on its way to Old Trafford.

For most of the season it seemed that Kevin Keegan's Newcastle United were going to win the race for the Championship - at one time they were twelve points clear at the top of the table, and I don't think many people outside of Manchester believed we had a hope of catching them...

The previous season, 1994-95, had been one of frustration and ultimately disappointment for me. I was carrying a hamstring injury during the later weeks of the Premiership campaign and I missed a number of games. My last one was in a 0-0 draw at home to Leeds on 2 April.

I played in the next two games, the FA Cup semi-final against Crystal Palace at Villa Park, a 2-2 draw, and the replay, also at Villa Park,

which we won 2-0 with goals from our heroic defensive duo Steve Bruce and Gary Pallister. The result took United into their thirteenth FA Cup final and the club's second 'double' was looking a distinct possibility if only we could catch up with, then overtake, Blackburn in the league.

Action from the opening game of the season, a defeat by Aston Villa

In the end the drama went right to the last day of the season, by which time we were within reach of Rovers. If we won the last game at West Ham, and if Liverpool beat Blackburn at Anfield, then we would be champions for the third time in succession.

Liverpool did beat Blackburn, 2-1, but we were held to a 1-1 draw at Upton Park – and the title went to Rovers. To say we were gutted would be an understatement.

Six days later came the FA Cup final against Everton. By then I was fit enough to be included in the squad and was named as one of the subs. By the time I was called on in place of Steve Bruce, we were a goal down, scored by Everton's Paul Rideout. Unfortunately we were unable to turn the game around and the scoreline remained the same.

This was my third Wembley final, but it was the first time I'd been on

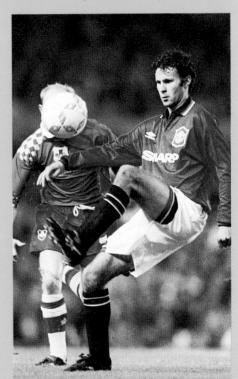

Coca-Cola Cup action against York City

9

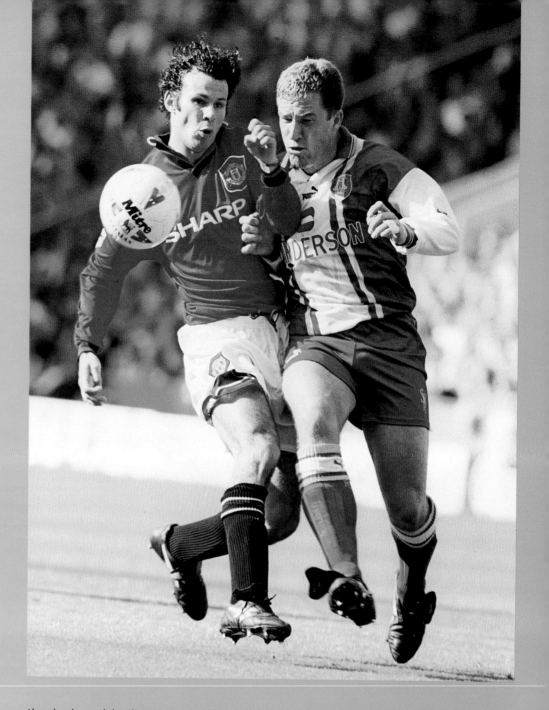

**Running into
Sheffield
Wednesday's
Pete Atherton**

the losing side. It was perhaps the biggest disappointments of my career.

Our only consolation was a place in the 1995-96 UEFA Cup competition, earned as a result of finishing second in the Premiership.

Throughout the close season I rested a lot, had regular treatment by the club's physios and went on a relaxing holiday. I started pre-season training but it was still hurting, so I rested some more and hoped that I'd be ready for the new campaign due to begin on 19 August with an away game at Aston Villa.

One of the great disappointments caused by my injury is that it ruled me out of contention for a place in the Welsh squad for the European Championship qualifier against Georgia at

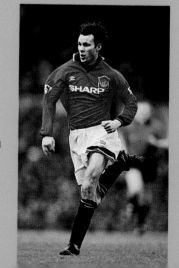

Cardiff Arms Park. Wales lost the game to a brilliant goal scored by Georgiou Kinkladze, who lobbed the ball over Neville Southall from all of twenty-five yards. It was a taste of things to come when the magical Georgiou arrived at Manchester City.

I was not ready to face Villa either at the start of the season.

You could say that we had done reasonably well in 1994-95 - but being second in two competitions was not really good enough for the players and fans of Manchester United. The world's greatest football club expects to win. And so we started the 1995-96 campaign with a new determination.

Mind you, our Premier League campaign got off to the worst possible start. Three of our top player of the previous season had gone.

United delight at a Paul Scholes goal

My good mate Paul Ince was in Italy with Inter Milan, Andrei Kanchelskis was on his way (eventually!) to Everton, and Mark Hughes had gone to Chelsea. And, of course, United's most influential player, Eric Cantona, was still serving the ban imposed after the infamous incident at Crystal Palace of the previous January.

The club was also affected by one or two other injuries and it was a drastically altered team that took to the field against ASTON VILLA at Villa Park. We were 3-0 down by half time and it wasn't until the last ten minutes that David Beckham supplied the one bright spot of the afternoon for United, by scoring our first goal of the season.

Things began to look up in the next game against WEST HAM UNITED at Old Trafford. We won 2-1, with a goal from Paul Scholes and the winner from Roy Keane. It was a touch of sweet revenge for that draw at Upton Park three months earlier, which had cost us the title.

By the time of our third game, against WIMBLEDON - who had started with two straight victories - I was reasonably fit again, and was named as sub by Alex Ferguson. In the 71st minute, when we 2-1 ahead, he sent me on as a replacement for Andy Cole who had scored our second goal.

I felt reasonably okay, and even more so when Roy Keane tapped home our third goal after a Lee Sharpe shot had been deflected to him off the Dons' 'keeper Paul Heald.

I was a late substitute in the next game, against champions BLACKBURN ROVERS at

Paul Scholes has just scored against Southampton

Ewood Park. We won 2-1, with goals from Lee Sharpe and David Beckham - and the season was starting to look pretty good for Manchester United.

I was on the bench again in the match against EVERTON at Goodison Park - and I was itching to get into the action. The scoreline stood at 2-2 by the time I was sent on in the 66th minute, in place of Paul Scholes - Lee Sharpe had scored both of our goals.

It was a very satisfying moment in the 73 minute when I was able to capitalise on a mistake in the Everton defence to score my first goal of the season - and United's winner.

It was the third time in the campaign that we had notched up victories over teams who had contributed most to our failure of the previous season - West Ham, Blackburn and Everton.

On Tuesday 12 September I was in United's starting line-up for the first time, in the UEFA Cup First Round first-leg against ROTOR VOLGOGRAD who had finished fourth in the previous season's Russian league table. It was a very tough game and Volgograd were a good team. We should have won but we managed to come away with a 0-0 draw, which was a good result, and we felt confident of beating them back on our own turf in the return leg.

Southampton's Ken Monkou and Eric Cantona in a chase for the ball

That weekend I played my first full Premiership game, against newly promoted BOLTON WANDERERS at Old Trafford. We played really well and I was feeling great. After about a quarter of an hour the Bolton defence failed to clear a cross which I'd put in from the left. Like lightning, Paul Scholes pounced on the ball and knocked it in.

**On the
ball
against
Chelsea**

In the 33rd minute Paul repaid the compliment by supplying me with a cross from the right which I was able to slide in at the near post for our second goal.

Paul wrapped up a brilliant afternoon when he rounded off the score at 3-0 with five minutes to go. The result took us to second place in the Premiership table, behind Kevin Keegan's Newcastle who had recently made their first slip up of the season when they were beaten by Southampton.

Next came a disaster in the the Second Round first-leg of the Coca-Cola Cup when we took on YORK CITY at Old Trafford. Despite loads of attacking from us - we had ten corners to their one - we were soundly beaten 3-0 by the Second Division side who played really well and deserved their success. Nevertheless it went down in the record books as our poorest home performance in three seasons.

The mood of despair must have stayed with us that Saturday when we went to SHEFFIELD WEDNESDAY and didn't play particularly well - although we did come away with a point from a 0-0 draw.

ROTOR VOLGOGRAD came to Old Trafford for the return leg of the UEFA Cup tie on 27 September. Unfortunately we put up a poor first half display and allowed them to score twice. We got back into the game after a while and were looking really good, back to top form almost, and

Mark Hughes in action for Chelsea against his old club

we pulled it back to 2-2 with goals from Paul Scholes and, incredibly, Peter Schmeichel - but they weren't enough and Volgograd progressed on the away goals ruling to meet Bordeaux in the next round.

The match against LIVERPOOL at Old Trafford on Sunday 1 October was a special occasion for all United fans, as it saw the return to action of Eric Cantona. And he was on top form, scoring the equaliser from the penalty spot in the 70th minute.

Nicky Butt had opened our account in the first minute of the match, from a chance created by Eric. But then Liverpool had got back into the game and two goals by hot-shot Robbie Fowler had given them the lead. It was after I'd been fouled in the box that Eric stepped up to fire us level from the spot. The points were shared - and King Eric was back where he belonged.

Two days later Eric lined-up with us to face YORK CITY in the return leg of the Coca-Cola Cup tie at a packed Bootham Crescent. We

knew what was needed and we tore into York from the off. A fine pass from Eric created our first goal in the sixth minute when Paul Scholes ran on to score from ten yards. We scored again seven minutes later through Terry Cooke.

But then Scott Jordan pulled one back for the home side in the 40th minute, which meant we had to score twice more to win. Unfortunately, we were only able to score one more goal, through Paul Scholes, as York battened down the hatches to hold on for a well-deserved giant killing victory.

We were now out of two cup competitions and hoping that the FA Cup would provide better fortune.

My next appearance in a red shirt, was for Wales against GERMANY in a European Championship Group 7 qualifier at Cardiff

Paul Parker challenges Leeds United's Tomas Brolin

Arms Park on 11 October. Wales were already out of contention for a place in England in the summer of '96 and Germany were set on powering their way to the finals.

It was a really good game and we were playing particularly well. Then in the 74th minute Andy Melville was unfortunate to score an own-goal to give Germany the lead. But we came back at them and levelled the score through Kit Symons four minutes later.

Unfortunately, the brilliant Jurgen Klinsmann was on hand to grab the winner for Germany with nine minutes to go.

After the game, I received a very flattering compliment from the German team boss Berti Vogts, when he said, "I wish Ryan Giggs had a German passport."

Our next Premiership game was the local derby with MANCHESTER CITY at Old Trafford. City were having a tough time of it and were stuck at the foot of the table with only a single point from eight games. And I'm afraid we made it worse for them, by winning 1-0. The goal came from our top scorer Paul Scholes from one of my corner-kicks.

Around this time there was talk of the Dutch winger Marc Overmars coming to Old Trafford from Ajax. Unfortunately, the move didn't come off because he was injured and would be out for the rest of the season.

On 21 October we played CHELSEA at Stamford Bridge and came away with three points in the bag after a brilliant 4-1 win. I got on the score sheet with our third goal. Scholsey scored twice and the other came from Brian McClair. Our old team-mate Mark Hughes, who had moved south to Stamford Bridge in the summer, got Chelsea's goal. The result kept us in touch with league leaders Newcastle, who were four points in front.

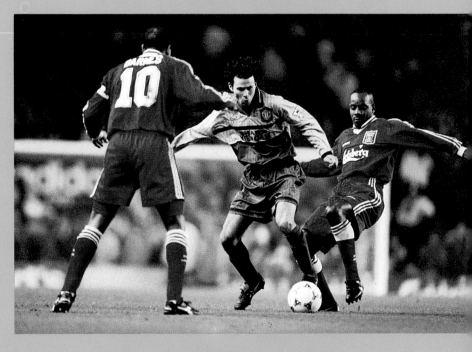

The Man in Grey takes on the Liverpool defence

It was nice to see Bryan Robson's return to Old Trafford on 28 October, as manager of MIDDLESBROUGH who were then lying fourth in the Premiership table.

After half an hour a hard task was made harder when Roy Keane was sent-off following a tussle with Jan-Aage Fjortoft. Amazingly we seemed to play better with ten men and shortly before half time I took a corner which Gary Walsh punched away, only to meet the head of Gary Pallister who scored from ten yards (against his old club).

With three minutes left Andy Cole got his second goal of the season when he latched onto an Eric Cantona pass and put the ball through Gary Walsh's legs.

That was our last match in October and it took us to within a point of Newcastle, although they still had a game in hand.

November started badly for United, with a 1-0 defeat at ARSENAL on the 4th. The goal which separated the two sides was scored by Dutch star Dennis Bergkamp after fifteen minutes.

But it was a great game in which we mounted attack after attack. Unfortunately they all resulted in nothing and set back our challenge on Newcastle.

Around this time we heard the news that Roy Keane, who was already suspended following his sending-off against Middlesbrough, would be our for weeks as he needed another hernia operation. This too was a setback.

On 15 November I played for Wales in ALBANIA in our final Group 7 European Championship qualifier. We were a goal down after just five minutes when they scored from the penalty spot. Just before half time we got back in it when Mark Pembridge headed home my cross for the equaliser.

But there were to be no more goals in the game, although we had two disallowed, and I went close on a couple of occasions.

It was back to Premiership action that weekend when SOUTHAMPTON came to Old Trafford. This time I didn't miss. In fact, I scored in the very first minute of the game (I'm told it was one of the quickest goals ever witnessed at Old Trafford) and again three minutes later.

Paul Scholes added another on eight minutes and after that onslaught there was little The Saints could do to catch us up. They did

The clash with table-toppers Newcastle

score through Neil Shipperley late in the second half, but by then Andy Cole had added our fourth. We were in great form that day.

A few days later we took on Ron Atkinson's COVENTRY CITY at Highfield Road. Once again we were in top form and produced four goals - from Denis Irwin, David Beckham and Brian McClair who scored twice. The whole team played brilliantly. I thoroughly enjoyed the game and was involved in the build-up to the first two goals.

NOTTINGHAM FOREST were our next opponents at the City Ground, on 27 November, two days before my 23rd birthday. Another four goals would have made a nice present, but we had to settle for a 1-1 draw. Paul McGregor opened the scoring for Forest on 19 minutes, and we did not equalise until the 66th minute when Eric Cantona scored from the penalty spot after he'd been brought down.

I picked up an injury at the City Ground and missed the next two Premiership matches - a 1-1 draw with CHELSEA and a 2-2 draw with SHEFFIELD WEDNESDAY, both played at Old Trafford. Eric Cantona scored both goals against Wednesday, including a brilliant late equaliser that really saved the day for us.

I was fit again in time for the match against LIVERPOOL on 17 December at Anfield. We didn't play well at all, and we deserved to lose. Robbie Fowler played a great game for Liverpool and ended up scoring two goals against us for the second time in the season as we lost 2-0.

On Christmas Eve we lost again, this time by a 3-1 margin to LEEDS UNITED at Elland Road. The only bright spot for us in a dull afternoon for us was Andy Cole's goal on the half hour.
The Leeds match was the first of a hectic period for Man United. Christmas is the busiest time of year for us players, when we play something like four games in seven days. This means we can't enjoy the holiday period like everyone else. There's no Christmas turkey washed down with wine for us. In fact, we trained on Christmas morning and then had the rest of the day to ourselves. That's when I exchange presents with my family!

On Wednesday 27 December, at Old Trafford,

we bounced right back to top form for our biggest game of the season so far. The match was against NEWCASTLE UNITED who were now leading the table by ten points. We had to win to keep in touch with them.

It was a great game - for us - we were one-up after just five minutes. I'd collected the ball in our own half and taken it on a long run into their half. Then I released it to Andy Cole on the edge of the box. Coley did the business and slotted it home. Roy Keane was playing a blinder that day, and it was he who notched our second goal early in the second half after David Beckham's pass had found him unmarked on the edge of the box. The 2-0 victory cut Newcastle's lead to seven points and we were in confident mood.

What A Wonderful Season continues on page 38

QUEENS PARK RANGERS were our last visitors of 1995. They had been down in the drop zone for most of the season and were desperate for points.

Our team included another French player, William Prunier, a defender on trial from Bordeaux. He played reasonably well against QPR and Andy Cole scored his third goal in three game to put us ahead just before half time.

Early in the second period I received a great cross from Denis Irwin and scored from about twelve yards out. Rangers replied with a later goal from Daniele Dichio, but the points were ours.

This meant we ended 1995 in second place behind Newcastle. They had 45 points from 20 games, we had 41 from 21.

It was going to be an interesting New Year.

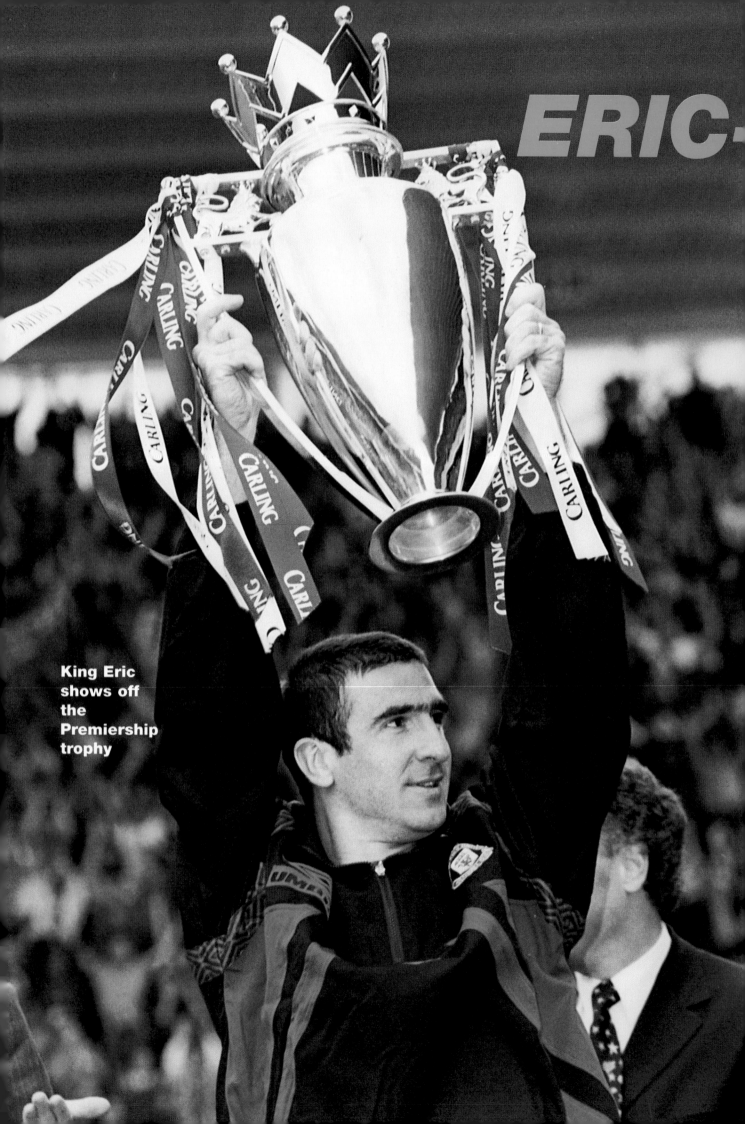

ERIC-

King Eric shows off the Premiership trophy

KING of OLD TRAFFORD

It could be argued that in 1994-95 Manchester United lost the title race due to Eric Cantona's ban, enforced by the authorities after that notorious 'kung fu' incident at Crystal Palace.

The ban meant Eric was out of action for eight months. He came back into United's team in the Premiership match against Liverpool at Old Trafford on 1 October 1995, and he scored the equaliser from the penalty spot.

For the remainder of the season, he continued to exert his formidable influence over the team and we became a more cohesive unit because of it.

His goals often provided vital victories on our run in to the Premiership title. And, of course, a moment of Cantona magic won us the FA Cup against Liverpool at Wembley - taking United to a special place in the history of English football, as the only club ever to win the 'double double'.

He also displayed a new calmness, and was not so volatile as he had been. He just got on with the job and even stepped in as skipper whenever Steve Bruce was out of the side.

Eric is quite simply the most talented individual I've ever played with - I've learnt so much from him. And I hope the lessons continue into the future.

Newcastle's Steve Howey gets to grips with Eric Cantona

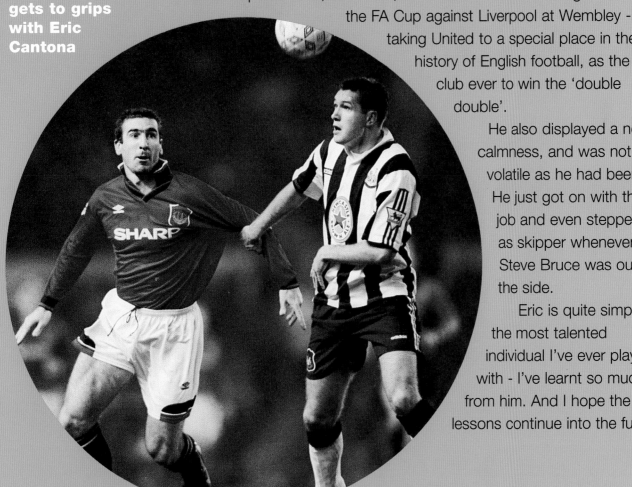

FERGIE - THE BOSS
who did the 'DOUBLE' TWICE

The Gaffer gets his hands on the Premier League Trophy again

Manchester United's boss Alex Ferguson the man who gave me my big break in the game is now the most successful soccer manager actively working in England today.

Before he came to Old Trafford in 1986, he had been successful as a player and then a manager in Scotland. In the early-80s he had led Aberdeen to a number of successes, including a memorable defeat of Real Madrid in the 1983 European Cup-Winners' Cup final, and he broke the 'Glasgow monopoly' held by Rangers and Celtic.

He arrived at Old Trafford when Ron Atkinson moved on, and set about building Manchester United into the greatest footballing force in the country. It took a while for Fergie's first trophy to arrive - the FA Cup in 1990 but it was the beginning of the club's Glory Years.

The European Cup-winners' Cup followed in 1991, after that great win in the finals against Barcelona. In 1992 United reached the final of the League Cup - then in 1993 after 26 years of frustration the club won the League Championship, a campaign of which I was proud to be a part, and which brought me my first major trophy.

Mine's a double!

It went on from there of course, with the double in 1993-94 and again last season.

Alex Ferguson really is a good boss to work for. He knows his players and he knows how to get the very best out of them.

I hope we do well in Europe in 1996-97 especially for him...

Ryan's Routine

Monday to Friday

Everything a professional footballer does obviously revolves around the matches he plays. Everything is geared to those 90 minute spells of pure excitement and action.

This means keeping fit and looking after yourself, eating the right food, getting enough proper rest and so on.

It also means training. At Manchester United we train every day of the week, providing we haven't got a midweek game. The training is conducted by club coach Brian Kidd and takes place at The Cliff, the club's second home, which is almost as famous as Old Trafford itself.

MONDAY is quite a easy day, especially if we've had a match on the previous Saturday or Sunday. Thankfully the training is always relatively light after a weekend game.

TUESDAY is probably the hardest day of the week in training. That's when we do a lot of running and a lots of fitness and stamina-building work - and we always go home feeling shattered on a Tuesday!

WEDNESDAY is quite a hard day as well, we play a lot of five-a-side games and a lot of other training games which Brian Kidd has seen on his travels abroad. He always makes these sessions very interesting and varied.

THURSDAY is usually taken up with shooting practice which gives everyone, especially the 'keepers, a lot of work to do.

FRIDAY is another relatively easy day's training. A warm-up is followed by a five-a-side game - the Young Lad v the Older Lads. I'm still a member of the Young Lads side, but Manchester United produces so many brilliant up-and-coming youngsters, that I'll soon be playing for the other lot! Friday's usually conclude with Alex Ferguson going over the tactics for the forthcoming match.

My **WARM-UP** routine before a match involves a lot of stretching to warm up the hamstrings. Because of the way I play I tend to do a lot more running than other players, so it is important that I warm-up properly.

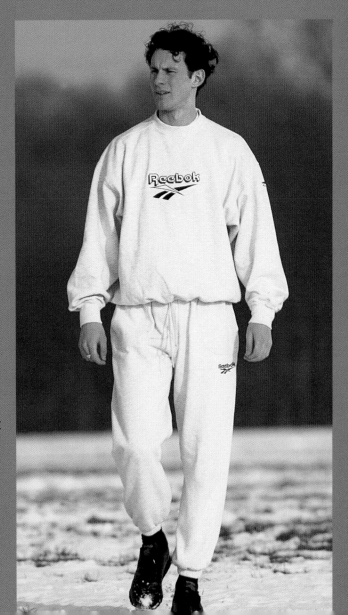

Here are some great portraits of Ryan taken on a snowy day in Manchester

Gallery...

My Team Mates

Peter Schmeichel

I'm really lucky to be playing for Manchester United. It is a wonderful football club, with a marvellous, unbelievable stadium, a terrific fan following and an incredible history. I can't imagine playing for anyone else.

Of course any club, however famous, is only as good as its team. And Alex Ferguson has gathered together some of the finest players in the modern game at Manchester United – a fact borne out by the success he has achieved.

Last season, when we started off without three of our top players Paul Ince, Mark Hughes and Andrei Kanchelskis, who all moved to other clubs, a lot of people predicted this would be the downfall of Man United.

But, under Alex Ferguson's guidance, the club seems to have a knack of producing good young players to slot effortlessly in alongside the more established stars and that's what happened in 1995-96...

Look at any successful football team and you'll always find a good goalkeeper at the back. Ours is PETER SCHMEICHEL the big Dane who is probably the best in the world. It gives a marvellous feeling of confidence to know there is someone of his calibre between the posts.

Goalkeepers are generally a bit crazy and Peter is no exception. He shouts a lot on the pitch when keeping his defence in order. (Come to think of it, he yells a lot off the pitch too!). He suffered a few knocks last season but soon bounced back to his very best, making his usual vital contributions to United's efforts.

GARY NEVILLE has done brilliantly since coming into the side. He was playing in the Manchester United Reserves team a couple of years ago, now he commands a place in the England team. Gary is a player

Phil
Neville

Gary
Neville

Gary
Pallister

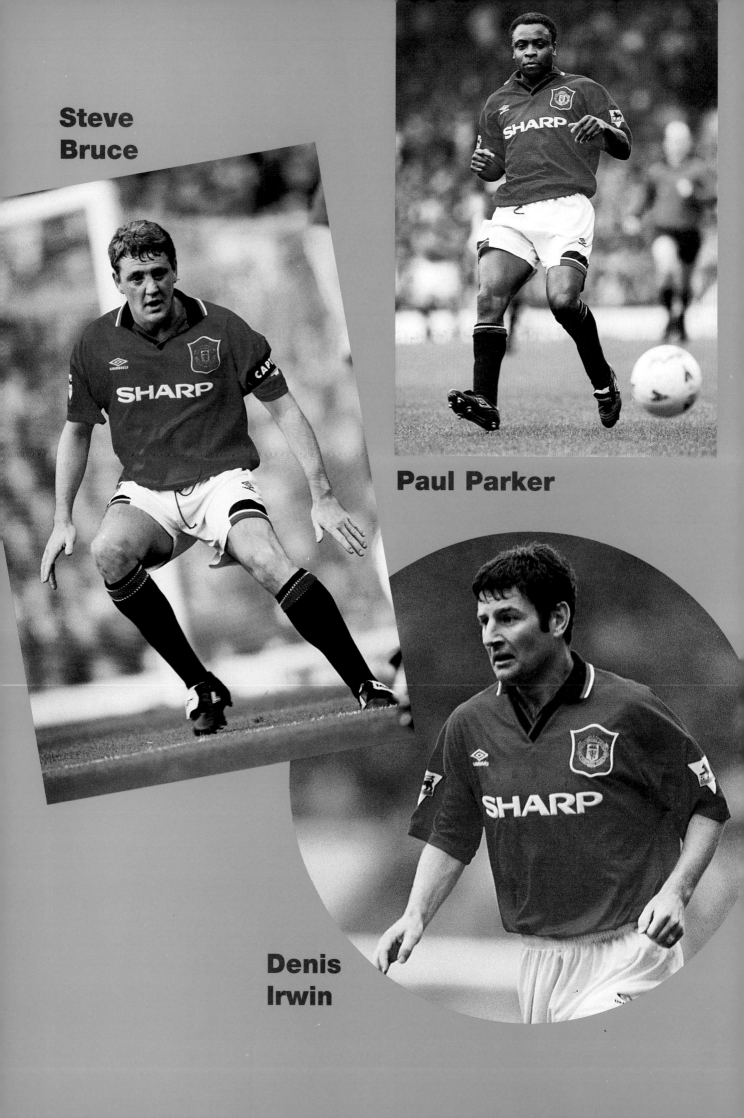

Steve Bruce

Paul Parker

Denis Irwin

who has matured very quickly a the highest level.

His brother, PHIL NEVILLE, is another great player and last season they became the first brothers called up for England since Jack and Bobby Charlton in the 1960s.

GARY PALLISTER was injured for a while last season. He has a back problem, but I reckon it's because at 6' 4" he's just too long!

He is a marvellous defender for Manchester United and England, and for a long timer he has been the other half of the incredible central defensive partnership with STEVE BRUCE. We were all sorry to see Brucie go off to Birmingham City, but I think a move was on the cards for him. During last season Wolves had approached him as a potential player/manager. But he was far to valuable to United's cause and, quite rightly, Alex Ferguson refused to let him go at that time. He certainly has all the qualities and experience to become a good manager one day. But meanwhile he still has a lot of playing to do with Brum under Trevor Francis' managership.

DENIS IRWIN has been Manchester United's most consistent player during the last few seasons. He's Mr Dependable, and he hardly ever puts a foot wrong. He might be the 'quiet man' of the team but believe me he's full of fire when it counts.

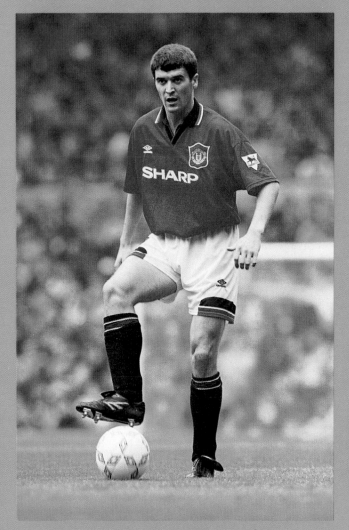

Roy Keane

It was also good to see PAUL PARKER back in the team, although he only made a handful of appearances. He had a lot of problems over the previous year. I think he was out for more than twelve months. Before that he was a regular in the England team and I'd say he's now in with a chance of getting back in.

ROY KEANE is a very influential midfield player for Manchester

United and the Republic of Ireland. He simply dominates everything around him and his battling qualities are well known. Whenever he's in the side he strengthens the midfield and gives it a more solid look.

Roy was out with a hernia for a while last season. But to demonstrate how important he, Jack Charlton still included him in the Republic of Ireland squad which played Holland in the European Championship play-off match at Anfield in December.

DAVID MAY was a brilliant player with Blackburn, and he's at last finding his feet at United. He scored a brilliant opening goal in the Premiership game against Middlesbrough on the day we won the title. He'd never been inured before he came to United, and then he met with a string of injuries. I'm sure he'll be a really good asset to United over the next few years.

NICKY BUTT has taken over in midfield from Paul Ince and he's done the job brilliantly. Butty's a contemporary of mine - we came up through the United ranks together and I hope we'll be playing alongside each other for years to come.

Nicky Butt

DAVID BECKHAM made a superb debut in 1994-95, but he only made a handful of appearances that season. Last time around he established himself in the side and scored a number of important goals into the bargain.

LEE SHARPE has been an Old Trafford star for a long time now. He was wanted by Spurs in January '96, but the bid was turned down by Alex Ferguson who knew how important Lee was to United.

BRIAN McCLAIR has been at United longer than any of us. He's

David Beckham

David May

Lee Sharpe

Brian McClair

Paul Scholes

Eric Cantona

been a marvellously consistent servant. He's the kind of player who can come in and play anywhere.

PAUL SCHOLES is a terrific goalscorer – 14 in the league and cups last season. He has even been compared to Old Trafford legend Denis Law. Paul is another player who has come up through the Manchester United youth ranks.

ERIC CANTONA is, of course, Manchester United's most influential player. He came back from that infamous ban last October and surprised everyone with his new, calm attitude. He took a lot of stick wherever he played but he just shrugged it off, got on with the job and steered us towards that 'double-double' with some great displays and some all-important goals.

Andy Cole

ANDY COLE has taken a little while to settle in at Old Trafford, rather like Stan Collymore has at Liverpool. But I know it will all come right for him in the end. He's still the fastest thing on two legs around Old Trafford. He's my room-mate too. He sleeps all the time and is a pretty quite sort of guy – especially when compared with my previous room mate Paul Ince who never stopped talking even his sleep!

Coley is a great goalscorer and although he hasn't yet reached the heights that he did with Newcastle a couple of season back, I know there are plenty more goals to come from him.

1995-96
WHAT A WONDERFUL SEASON -
Part two

The New Year began with a disaster for Manchester United. We were at TOTTENHAM, who were then playing very well and were challenging for a top three place .

We were still missing Steve Bruce and Gary Pallister at the back, and, to make matters worse, Peter Schmeichel somehow got injured in the the pre-match warm-up, but felt he was fit enough to play. Unfortunately, Peter was not as effective as usual and we were 2-1 down at half time. Andy Cole had scored our goal.

Kevin Pilkington took over from Peter for the second half, but it was Chris Armstrong's day he netted twice for Spurs to give them a 4-1 victory.

Five days later our FA Cup campaign began with the visit of SUNDERLAND to Old Trafford in the Third Round. Under Peter Reid's management, the Rokerites were then challenging for a play-off position in the First Division - they eventually went on to become champions and gain promotion to the Premiership.

Andy Cole on the attack against spurs

For most of the match they outplayed us, and we found ourselves 2-1 down with eleven minutes to go.

Thankfully Eric Cantona saved the day with a goal headed in at the far post with just eleven minutes to go. We had earned a replay at Roker Park.

Our title challenge resumed on 13 January with the visit of ASTON VILLA to Old Trafford. They put up a solid defensive display, with Paul McGrath at his best, and although we had most of the play we could not break them down. Likewise, they did not get much of a look-in at our goal, which was guarded by a fit-again peter Schmeichel, and it all ended in a 0-0 stalemate.

Next came the FA Cup Third Round replay

at SUNDERLAND. For most of the match it looked as though we might be making an early exit from the competition. Sunderland scored first after 24 minutes through Phil Gray while our defence was appealing for an offside decision.

It wasn't until late on that we got back into the game when Phil Neville set up Paul Scholes with a brilliant pass for the equaliser. Paul hadn't long been on as a sub for Nicky Butt and he drilled the ball past Alec Chamberlain in the Sunderland goal.

The home crowd had been giving Andy Cole some stick all night, for his previous association with their rivals Newcastle and his £7 million price tag. But he stunned them into silence in the last minute with a brilliantly headed match winning goal from a Lee Sharpe cross. We were through to the Fourth Round.

On the following Monday we travelled to East London for the

Eric Cantona celebrates his goal against West Ham

Premiership clash with WEST HAM. It was the first time we'd been back there since losing out on the title in the previous season's last game.

We started well, and on eight minutes I supplied the cross from which Eric Cantona opened the scoring. From then on it was a good old battle with the Hammers throwing everything at us in an effort to find an equaliser. But it didn't come and we took the much-needed three points. The only disappointment about the evening was the sending-off of Nicky Butt towards the end of the game, for a second bookable offence. And then, as the team coach was heading

back northwards we realised we were missing one very important member of our squad - Alex Ferguson - he'd been left behind and we had to go back for him!

We were back down south again on the following weekend, for the FA Cup Fourth Round game against READING at a packed Elm Park. Despite Reading's pre-match pep-talk from Uri Geller, it was us who demonstrated the power of positive thinking. Mind you, it took us half an hour or so to get into the game. The Royals went close a couple of times before we broke the deadlock when a Lee Sharpe shot rebounded to me off their goalkeeper Nicky Hammond - and I was able to hit the ball home.

After that, we were in command, with Roy Keane in top form in our midfield. Two more goals came, a 25-yarder from Paul Parker and a last-minute strike from Eric Cantona. It was on to the next round for United.

Premiership business resumed on 3 February when we were at Selhurst Park to take on WIMBLEDON. It was the first time Eric Cantona had been back to the ground where that unfortunate incident had occurred just over a year earlier. But it didn't bother him much, as he went on to score twice late in the match which we won 4-2.

Eric goes flying against Villa

Andy Cole had opened our account near to half time when he headed home a Denis Irwin cross. Our other goal was an 'OG' headed in by the Dons' Chris Perry after a David Beckham shot rebounded to him. David had come on as a sub when Steve Bruce was taken off injured.

The following weekend saw the visit of BLACKBURN ROVERS to Old Trafford. Once again we were the dominant team. Lee Sharpe was brilliant, and David May was an excellent stand-in for the injured Steve Bruce. Our goal came from Lee in the 14th minute when he hammered home an Andy Cole effort which had rebounded to him off the post. In the end, though, we felt we should have had more out of the game. But the three points were more than welcome - they kept us in touch with Newcastle.

On Sunday 18 February, and for the second time in the season, MANCHESTER CITY came to Old Trafford - this time in the FA Cup Fifth Round. With half time looming the scoreline stood at 1-0 to City. They had gone ahead through Uwe Rosler.

Flying against Wimbledon

Then I took a corner which I felt I'd hit a bit too long. Next thing I know, the referee had blown for a penalty. Even the United players who were close by didn't really know why it had been given, although Eric Cantona and Michael Frontzech had been involved in a minor skirmish inside the area. Anyway, Eric gratefully stepped up to take the spot kick and he sent Ike Immel the wrong way for the equaliser.

With the balance restored we came out for the second half with a new determination and we eventually broke them down with a winning goal in the 77th minute by the in form Lee Sharpe from a Phil Neville cross. And the Twin Towers began to look a bit closer!

Three days later EVERTON came to Old Trafford in the Premiership. It was a tough game, with the visitors putting up a good resistance, but Roy Keane got us off the mark on the half hour mark.

Our second goal was something special. The move started way back in our own half. Then Lee Sharpe, myself and Eric Cantona released Andy Cole down the left while I got forward. Andy supplied a brilliant cross and I hit it with my left foot from about twelve yards out then saw it beat Neville Southall in the Everton goal. Very satisfying!

The points took us closer to Newcastle who had recently lost at

West Ham. The following Saturday they only managed a draw at Manchester City and we felt they were well within our sights especially after our visit to Burnden Park on Sunday 25 February.

BOLTON WANDERERS had occupied bottom spot in the Premier League for most of the season, and were consequently tipped as the most likely to go down of all the relegation candidates . But, they had recently had their hopes raised with a win against Middlesbrough. I'm afraid we plunged them back into despair.

David May opens the scoring against Middlesbrough

... and then he celebrates

Our first goal came on five minutes when my shot hit the crossbar and rebounded to David Beckham who headed home. Ten minutes later Steve Bruce popped up to head his first goal of the season, from a David Beckham corner.

We were always in control of the game, but no more goals were forthcoming until twenty minutes from time, when Andy Cole got on the scoresheet after collecting a pass from Brian McClair, turning a defender and thumping the ball home off the underside of the bar.

Soon after that Paul Scholes came on as a sub for Eric Cantona and within six minutes of his arrival he'd scored two goals! The first came after he'd beaten a defender and slotted home a low shot past Keith Branagan – the second, when he diverted a Brian McClair effort into the net. But there was still more to come, in the shape of Nicky Butt who hit our sixth goal from an Andy Cole pass.

The 6-0 scoreline was Manchester United's best since we'd beaten Ipswich 9-0 in the previous season. More importantly the result took us to within four points of NEWCASTLE UNITED and they were our next opponents.

The Big Game took place on 4 March at St James' Park where The Magpies had not lost all season. And in the first half it looked as if it was going to stay that way. They were all over us and could have been two or three-nil ahead by the interval.

But we held on, and about six minutes into the second period Eric the Magician pulled another rabbit out of the hat when he put the finishing touch to a move created by Phil Neville and Andy Cole, to score the only goal of the game.

That was a brilliant result for us, and in the final analysis would prove to be the turning point of our season. The gap at the top was now down to a single point. Newcastle had 61 points, we had 60. They also had a game in hand, so it was absolutely vital that we kept producing good results.

But we next had to turn out attention to the FA Cup quarter-final tie against SOUTHAMPTON at Old Trafford on 11 March. By half time Southampton had had the ball in the net, but the referee disallowed Neil Shipperly's effort and we breathed again.

Andy Cole scores United's second against Middlesbrough

Five minutes into the second half Eric Cantona turned the game around with a 'tap in' goal from my low cross from the left. Lee Sharpe added our second in the last minute when he finished off a move involving Eric and Nicky Butt. We were into the semis!

Next came the Premiership game against QUEENS PARK RANGERS at Loftus Road - one

of my favourite away grounds because of the terrific atmosphere there. Rangers were in dire trouble down in the relegation zone and would eventually go down to the First Division. They almost took all three points, having gone ahead in the 63rd minute when a Daniele Dichio shot was deflected into our net by Denis Irwin as he attempted to head it away. But we kept plugging away and in the last minute I sent a cross over to Eric Cantona at the far post and he buried it for a share of the points.

The draw took us above Newcastle at the top of the table. Both teams had 61 points, but were separated by our slightly superior goal-difference. However, Newcastle still held the initiative as they had two games in hand.

An Eric Cantona goal, the only one of the game against ARSENAL at Old Trafford on 20 March, kept us in the title race. It was a brilliant goal, too - he first intercepted a clearance on his chest, then moved forward a couple of paces, before hitting the ball from all of 30-yards right into the top of the Gunners' net.

It was Eric's fourth goal in as many games - and each one had been vital to United's cause.

Four days later Arsenal's north-London neighbours, TOTTENHAM HOTSPUR came to Old Trafford next and yet again Eric Cantona scored the only goal of the game. It began in the 51st minute, from a goal-kick which was hotly disputed by the Spurs' players who felt they should have had a corner instead. Eric produced a magnificent individual run before firing in a left-foot shot from the edge of the area.

Two views of my goal against 'Boro

It was a great result, especially as Newcastle had slipped up with a 2-0 defeat by Arsenal on the previous day. We were now three points ahead.

The last day of March saw us in FA Cup semi-final action against Glenn Hoddle's CHELSEA at Villa Park. The Blues went ahead on 35 minutes through one of the season's most impressive players - Ruud Gullit. He headed home after a cross provided by ex-Man United hero Mark Hughes.

In the second half we fought back with Eric Cantona orchestrating things and David May and Gary Neville working wonders in the defence. The equaliser came in the 55th minute, when Eric headed the ball into the danger area and Andy Cole was on hand to thump it home.

David Beckham provided the winning goal five minutes later, when he latched on to a mis-hit clearance before firing a low drive past Kevin Hitchcock in the Chelsea goal. The result meant that we would meet Liverpool in the final at Wembley on 11 May.

And so we moved into April with the 'double' in our sights , although there was still a long way to go. First we had to overcome our neighbours MANCHESTER CITY at Maine Road. Alan Ball's team were still struggling, and were now hovering just above the drop zone. I'm afraid we did nothing to aid their cause as we took all three points with a 3-2 win.

Eric Cantona opened the scoring from the penalty-spot in the 7th

I get my hands on the Premiership trophy

Left:
Saluting United's fans at the end of the Premiership campaign

minute, after Denis Irwin had been brought down. Kavelashvili equalised on 39 minutes, but Andy Cole shot us ahead again three minutes later after conducting a neat one-two with Eric on the edge of the penalty-area.

In the 71st minute Uwe Rosler made it 2-2. And I was on hand to provide the winner from a hard struck 20-yarder, after Eric had supplied me with the pass that made it possible. The result kept us ahead in the title race. We now had 70 points, Newcastle had 67, but had a game in hand. Two days later the Magpies gave up that advantage when they were beaten 2-1 by Blackburn at Ewood Park on 8 April.

On the same day we were playing relegation-threatened COVENTRY CITY at Old Trafford. The match was barely two minutes old when it provided a reminder of just how precarious football can be. Coventry's defender David Buust was on a foray into our penalty area when he broke his leg in the most horrendous way and would obviously be facing many months of recuperation. We all felt really sorry for him, as there is nothing more frustrating for a professional footballer than being unable to play because of an injury.

The first half of the 'double' is in the bag

The match itself was won by a single goal, provided by the inevitable Monsieur Cantona who scored after the Sky Blues' defence had failed to clear my cross from the left. It was Eric's seventh goal in eight games, and United's fifteenth victory in sixteen matches.

Unfortunately, that run was about to come to an abrupt halt, on a particularly grey day for us, down at The Dell in the next league game against SOUTHAMPTON.

The Saints, who were battling for Premiership survival, put in a spirited display

and went a goal-up in the eleventh minute through Ken Monkou. By half-time they had added two more through Neil Shipperley and Matt Le Tissier.

At half time we changed our grey strip for the blue-and-white striped one as some of our team were complaining that the grey was blending in with the background and making it difficult to pick each other out.

The blue and white strip is far more striking and our performance did improve a bit in the second period. But we only scored one goal. It came a minute from time when Phil Neville pulled a great pass back to me and I was able to side-foot the ball home.

The defeat meant that the title race was wide open once again, especially when Newcastle beat Villa -1-0 on the following day.

We just had to knuckle down and get on with the next game, against LEEDS UNITED at Old Trafford on 17 April. Once again we won by a 1-0 margin, with the goal coming from Roy Keane in the 72nd minute. And not a moment too soon, as we already knew that Newcastle were beating Southampton by the same margin at St James' Park.

NOTTINGHAM FOREST came to Old Trafford on 28 April, for our last home game of 1995-96. The 53,926 crowd, the biggest of the season - the Premiership's biggest-ever, witnessed our biggest home victory of the campaign.

It began with two goals just before half time, from Paul Scholes and David Beckham. Then in the second half the floodgates opened to allow us three more goals, from David Beckham, myself and Eric Cantona. The 5-0

Brian Kidd and Alex Ferguson show off the trophy

result left us poised to take the Championship, even after Newcastle beat Leeds on the following day to keep up their title challenge. Both clubs had just one more game to play, but we were on 79 points, they were on 77.

If we won our last game against MIDDLESBROUGH at the Riverside Stadium we were champions. If we lost and Newcastle beat Tottenham at White Hart lane then the Magpies would take the title.

In the event Spurs held Newcastle to a 1-1 draw at White Hart Lane, while we dominated Bryan Robson's 'Boro to win 3-0 with goals from David May - his first of the season, - Andy Cole and finally, Ryan Giggs. It was a great way to tie up the Premiership campaign.

We were Champions again!

Beating Liverpool's Jamie Redknapp to the ball in the FA Cup final

But could we become the first ever club to win the coveted League and Cup 'double' for a second time? The answer to that question came on 11 May at Wembley, against LIVERPOOL.

The 1996 FA Cup final was a match dominated by nerves - and won by a moment of sheer genuis.

And who provided it? Yes, Eric Cantona.

His now famous goal came in the 86th minute when Liverpool 'keeper David James attempted to punch the ball clear and Eric was there, taking a step back before volleying the ball right back into the Liverpool net. It was a difficult goal to score, but he did it to perfection.

The result meant of course, that Manchester United had written a unique chapter in the soccer history books - as the only team ever to

Cup winners

win the English League and the FA Cup in the same season twice!

I am immensely proud to have been part of that success, and I congratulate all my team-mates and the Gaffer Alex Ferguson who brilliantly masterminded the whole thing.

We now have to see if we can establish ourselves among the top clubs in Europe. It was good to learn that this time United are among the 'seeded' teams in the Champions' Cup, which means that we go straight into the Champions' League rather than having to qualify. Whoever we are drawn against, you can rest assured that we'll be giving it our all. It's another challenge we will relish at Old Trafford.

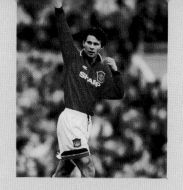

Showing off the trophies in the streets of Manchester

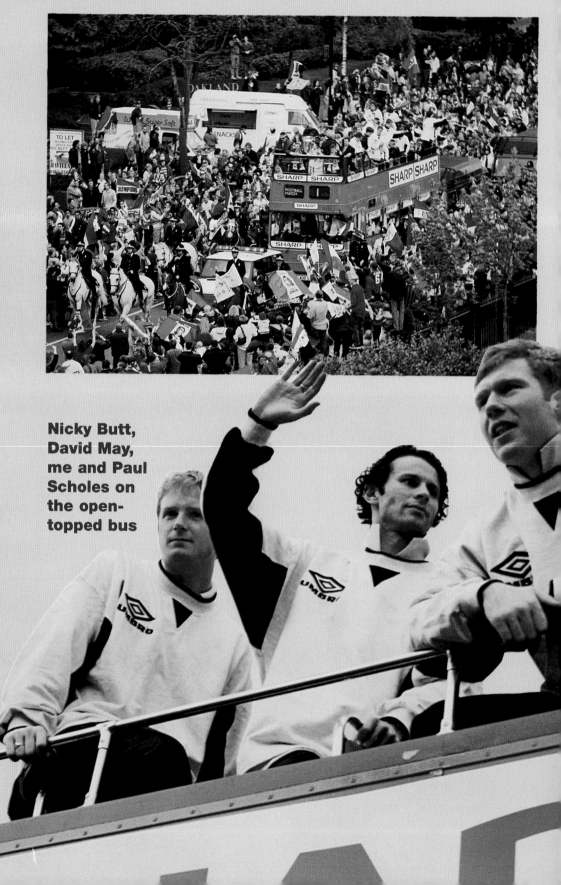

Nicky Butt, David May, me and Paul Scholes on the open-topped bus

The Double- the facts

UNITED'S ROUTE TO PREMIERSHIP GLORY 1995-96

AUGUST 1995
19th	v Aston Villa	(A)	1-3
23rd	v West Ham	(H)	2-1
26th	v Wimbledon	(H)	3-1
28th	v Blackburn R	(H)	2-1

SEPTEMBER
9th	v Everton	(A)	3-2
16th	v Bolton W	(H)	3-0
23rd	v Sheffield Wed	(A)	0-0

OCTOBER
1st	v Liverpool	(H)	2-2
14th	v Manchester C	(H)	1-0
21st	v Chelsea	(A)	4-1
28th	v Middlesbrough	(H)	2-0

NOVEMBER
4th	v Arsenal	(A)	0-1
18th	v Southampton	(H)	4-1
22nd	v Coventry C	(A)	4-0
27th	v Nottingham F	(A)	1-1

DECEMBER
2nd	v Chelsea	(H)	1-1
9th	v Sheffield W	(H)	2-2
17th	v Liverpool	(A)	0-2
24th	v Leeds U	(A)	1-3
27th	v Newcastle U	(H)	2-0
30th	v QPR	(H)	2-1

JANUARY 1996
1st	v Tottenham H	(A)	1-4
13th	v Aston Villa	(H)	0-0
22nd	v West Ham U	(A)	1-0

FEBRUARY
3rd	v Wimbledon	(A)	4-2
10th	v Blackburn R	(H)	1-0
21st	v Everton	(H)	2-0
25th	v Bolton W	(A)	6-0

MARCH
4th	v Newcastle U	(A)	1-0
16th	v QPR	(A)	1-1
20th	v Arsenal	(H)	1-0
24th	v Tottenham H	(H)	1-0

APRIL
6th	v Manchester C	(A)	3-2
8th	v Coventry C	(H)	1-0
13th	v Southampton	(A)	1-3
17th	v Leeds U	(H)	1-0
28th	v Nottingham F	(H)	5-0

MAY
| 5th | v Middlesbrough | (A) | 3-0 |

THE FA PREMIER LEAGUE FINAL TABLE 1995-96

	P	W	D	L	F	A	Pts
Manchester United	38	25	7	6	73	35	82
Newcastle United	38	24	6	8	66	37	78
Liverpool	38	20	11	7	70	34	71
Aston Villa	38	18	9	11	52	35	63
Arsenal	38	17	12	9	49	32	63
Everton	38	17	10	11	64	44	61
Blackburn Rovers	38	18	7	13	61	47	61
Tottenham Hotspur	38	16	13	9	50	38	61
Nottingham Forest	38	15	13	10	50	54	58
West Ham United	38	14	9	15	43	52	51
Chelsea	38	12	14	12	46	44	50
Middlesbrough	38	11	10	17	35	50	43
Leeds United	38	12	7	19	40	57	43
Wimbledon	38	10	11	17	55	70	41
Sheffield Wednesday	38	10	10	18	48	61	40
Coventry City	38	8	14	16	42	60	38
Southampton	38	9	11	18	34	52	38
Manchester City	38	9	11	18	33	58	38
Queens Park Rangers	38	9	6	23	38	57	33
Bolton Wanderers	38	8	5	25	39	71	29

UNITED'S ROUTE TO FA CUP GLORY IN 1996

6.1.96	Third Round	v Sunderland (H)	2-2
16.1.96	Third Round Replay	v Sunderland (A)	2-1
27.1.96	Fourth Round	v Reading (A)	3-0
18.2.96	Fifth Round	v Manchester City (H)	2-1
11.3.96	Sixth Round	v Southampton (H)	2-0
31.3.96	Semi-final	v Chelsea (Villa Park)	2-1
11.5.96	Final	v Liverpool (Wembley)	1-0

THE Ryan Giggs STORY

By TONY LYNCH

An early
appearance
in United's
colours

Ryan Joseph Giggs, a child destined to become one of the best footballers ever produced by his country, was born on Thursday 29 November 1973, in Cardiff, the capital city of Wales.

He was known as Ryan Wilson then. His father, Danny Wilson, was a well-known professional Rugby League player. His mum, Lynne, is the daughter of a policeman. When Ryan was a youngster his dad signed for Swinton Rugby League Club, situated in the suburbs of Manchester, and the family moved northwards. That's why the young Welsh boy grew up with a Manchester accent, but he would never forget his roots in the Land of Song!

Following in his father's footsteps, Ryan was a promising rugby player as a lad – a speedy stand-off who played in a local lads' team and was once reckoned to be good enough to be a Great Britain trialist at junior level.

Giggsy about to score against Spurs at White Hart Lane

But his real love was soccer. He was a good player right from the start. As a young schoolboy he played for the Salford Boys' XI and was invited to train with Manchester City at their School of Excellence where he went twice a week.

News of the promising youngster quickly spread among the clubs of the north-east, and he was watched by scouts from Blackburn, Blackpool and Preston, among others. But he always thought that Manchester City would eventually ask him to become an associated schoolboy.

That never happened - which, looking back, has to go down as an astonishing oversight on the part of the Maine Roaders!

Instead the 14 year-old Giggs was surprised one day by a visit from the Manchester United's manager Alex Ferguson who asked if he would like to become an associated schoolboy at Old Tafford.

In truth, young Giggsy had been Man-U-Mad ever since his father had first taken him to watch a game at Old Trafford when he was seven. But first, and out of politeness, Ryan's mum asked City if they would be asking him to join them. When they said no, the coast was clear for United.

Manchester United has one of the best

youth development systems in Britain and Ryan found himself among players of his own level. But still he shone as a outstanding young prospect. So much so, that United's director and former star Bobby Charlton was once heard to mutter, "Thank God we've got him!"

When Ryan was sixteen he was offered a traineeship with the club. Alex Ferguson said, "He's the best I've ever seen at that age."

By then Giggsy had captained the England Schoolboys team (schoolboys represent the country they live in, not the one in which they were born). He quickly worked his way up through the Manchester United ranks - Youth team, 'B' team, 'A' team, Reserves.

Then, in March 1991, when he was 17, he was included in United's squad for the

A Ryan Giggs free-kick against Ipswich Town

League match against Everton at Goodison Park. Before the match he was named as one of the substitutes, and during the game Alex Ferguson sent him on in place of Denis Irwin.

The wily Ferguson was gradually giving Giggsy experience of life in the top flight. His next appearance, in the local derby against Manchester City, was notable as the match in which Ryan scored his first goal for United. It came in the 22nd minute during a goalmouth scramble, although Ryan later said the ball simply rebounded of him and a defender before going into the City goal. Nevertheless, his name was on the scoresheet at last, and that is a massive confidence booster for any young footballer.

In May 1991 Ryan received his first international call-up by Wales and played in the Under-21 victory over Poland. Five months later he would find himself the youngest Welsh full international debutant of all time.

In 1991-92 his chance to impress further, came when Lee Sharpe was ruled out through

injury. Giggs stepped into the left wing berth, and stayed there for most of the season as Manchester United looked set to become League Champions. In the end they lost out to Leeds United who pipped them at the post.

That season did bring Ryan's first major honour, as United lifted the Coca-Cola Cup, beating Nottingham Forest 1-0 in the final. He was also voted the 1992 Young Player of the Year by the members of the Professional Footballers' Association.

1992-93 was a magnificent season for Manchester United and Ryan Giggs. It was the first season of the brand new FA Premier League and it brought United's first Championship in 26 years. Giggsy had been a major player in the drama, and his efforts were rewarded with a second PFA Young Player of the Year Award – the first time any

Scoring for Wales

Congratulations from Darren Ferguson

footballer had won that particular trophy twice.

In 1993-94 United did even better than in the previous campaign, when they became only the sixth English club ever to achieve the League and FA Cup 'double'. They lost only four matches in the Premiership campaign and won the title eight points ahead of closest rivals Blackburn Rovers.

In the FA Cup final at Wembley, Ryan was in the United team that

met Chelsea who were the only side to have beaten them twice earlier in the season - but it wasn't to happen again. United won the match 4-0 after a stunning second half display in which the mercurial Eric Cantona scored two penalties.

By comparison the following season 1994-95 was a disappointing one for Manchester United and for Ryan Giggs. Once again they were involved in the thick of things and right up there in the race for the Premiership title. But they lost the race on the last day and Blackburn Rovers took the title.

United also reached the FA Cup final - for their third Wembley appearance in three years. This time, however, they were beaten by Everton and so finished as runners-up in both major competitions.

Close attention from Tottenham defenders in 1993

Ryan was injured towards the end of that campaign, and appeared as substitute in the Cup final. Then he took his summer break, before embarking on the remarkable 1995-96 'double-double' campaign which he tells us all about elsewhere in this Annual.

Remarkably Ryan is still only 23 years-old, and he already has a

collection of honours that any professional footballer would be proud of Yet, it is incredible to think that Giggsy's Golden Years may be yet to come.

Here come United!

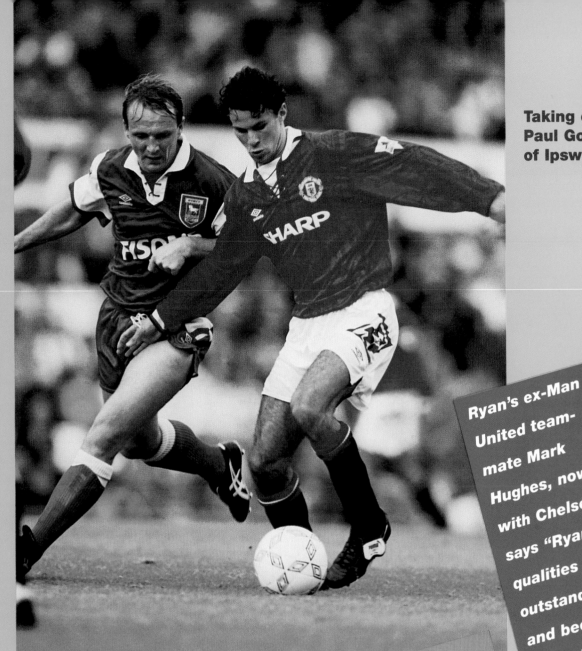

Ryan's ex-Man United team-mate Mark Hughes, now with Chelsea, says "Ryan's qualities are outstanding and because of his ability it's easy to forget how young he is. He must be murder to play against."

Ryan has often been compared to George Best, the great Manchester United and Northern Ireland winger of the 1960s and '70s. Indeed, the two men do share many of the same qualities speed, skill and perfect balance. And, just like George, Ryan is as tough as old boots when it counts.

Giggsy

AT A GLANCE

Full Name: Ryan Joseph Giggs
Date of Birth: 29 November 1973
Birthplace: Cardiff
Height: 5' 11"
Weight: 10st 9lbs

Signed for Manchester United:
1 December 1990, after traineeship
First Team Debut: v Everton (sub) on 2 March 1991
First League Goal: v Manchester City on 4 May 1991

HONOURS
FA Premier League Championship:
1992-93, 1993-94, 1995-96
FA Cup : 1994, 1996
Coca-Cola Cup: 1992
Charity Shield: 1993, 1994
English Schools Cup: 1991
FA Youth Cup: 1992
PFA Young Player of the Year: 1992, 1993

INTERNATIONAL
Wales: Youth, Under-21, Full
England: English Schoolboys' Captain

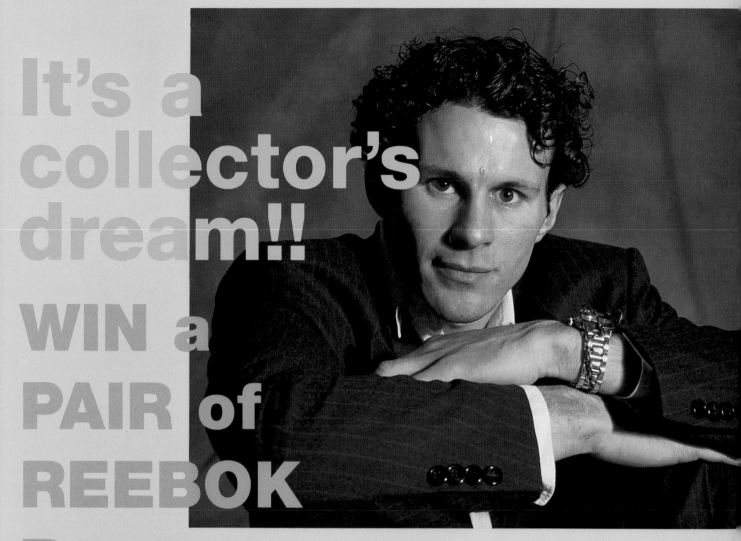

It's a
collector's
dream!!
WIN a
PAIR of
REEBOK
Boots
Actually
worn
by RYAN
GIGGS!

COMPETITION

The winner of this great competition will receive a pair of Reebok boots actually worn by Ryan Giggs!

All you have to do is answer these three simple questions:

1. Against which team did Ryan score Manchester United's last Premier League goal of 1995-96?

2. Who were Manchester United's FA Cup final opponents when they first achieved the 'double' in 1993-94?

3. In which city was Ryan Giggs born?

Write your answers on a postcard or the back of a sealed-down empty envelope, included your name age and address, and post to:

Ryan Giggs Competition
Grandreams Ltd
Jadwin House
205-211 Kentish Town Road
London NW5 2JU

Closing date for entries is 31st March 1997

A pair of Reebok boots worn by Ryan Giggs will be sent to the sender of the first all correct entry drawn out of the bag on the closing date. The publishers decision is final and no correspondence will be entered into.

BOBBY CHARLTON
HEALTH & FITNESS CENTRE
061-653 2070